No More Fear for Kids

A 40-day devotional for parents and kids
to work together to conquer worry

JoHannah Reardon

DEDICATION

To my grandchildren—may you learn to
conquer your fears early in life!

Note to Parents

If you are fearful and anxious, you may be able to mask it very well for years, as I did. In fact, you may mask it so well that you don't even recognize it as being a problem, but it will eventually catch up with you and affect your emotional, spiritual, and physical well being.

Once I recognized my own anxiety, I began to see it everywhere, in everyone. Interestingly, it has been easiest to see in the children I am around. As we mature, most of us learn to tamp down our anxiety so it's invisible to the world—and often to ourselves—but children have not yet learned that skill.

When I pointed out some poison ivy to my grandson, he was suddenly uncontrollably itchy all over, even though we were nowhere near it and he hadn't touched it. I thought this was ridiculous until I began thinking about how I often do the same thing. For example, when a friend of mine found out she had cancer, I began experiencing some of the symptoms she had, causing me all sorts of unnecessary fear. As Michel de Montaigne, an influential writer of the French Resistance, said, "He who fears he shall suffer, already suffers what he fears."

When my three-year-old granddaughter wouldn't go into my basement because there might be lions down there, I laughed at the ridiculousness of her irrational fear. But then I began thinking about all the times I'd imagined someone lurking in a dark alley waiting to spring at me. In a sense, our fears are not different at all.

I recently talked to a middle-school student who'd joined the track team. She loved the practices, but on days they had a meet, she would become so anxious she felt like throwing up. Her friends had similar reactions when they had to give a speech or take a standardized test.

They all thought it was great to run with or chat with friends, but it was another thing to compete with them for a trophy or a grade.

Fear also dictates what a child will try. She'd like to go out for that team, sign up to play an instrument, ride that roller coaster, and so on, but stepping into the unknown means she might fail . . .

There are endless things for kids to fear these days. When adults talk about the future grimly, kids have trouble feeling hopeful about what is ahead. Fear and worry are nothing new, but today our knowledge of all the bad that is happening in the world multiplies our anxiety exponentially. We have informational access to all the disasters of the world but are limited by time and space to do anything about them. We are bombarded daily with needs we can't meet and evil we can't comprehend, and it's hard not to let our own fears and worries drift down to our children.

Parenting brings it's own set of fears. At times it's terrifying to think we are responsible for other tiny humans who seem so vulnerable and easily wounded. As parents, we can become frightened beyond all reason as we try to protect these fragile creatures given to our care. We fear our children will come to physical or emotional harm, and our kids sense this, which adds to their own fears.

I'm convinced that children who battle fear the most are those with a good imagination. It's easy for them to picture all the things that can go wrong and all the unknowns that can threaten them.

So What's the Answer?

The first step is to help our children recognize their fears and anxieties. Only when they see them for what they are can they begin to put them in their proper place. Yann Martel wrote a book called *Life of Pi*, which is fictional tale about a man stuck in a small boat with a tiger. The main character of this tale says:

> "I must say a word about fear. It is life's only true opponent. Only fear can defeat life. It is a clever, treacherous adversary, how well I know. It has no decency, respects no law or convention, shows no mercy. It goes for your weakest spot,

which it finds with unnerving ease. It begins in your mind, always . . . so you must fight hard to express it. You must fight hard to shine the light of words upon it. Because if you don't, if your fear becomes a wordless darkness that you avoid, perhaps even manage to forget, you open yourself to further attacks of fear because you never truly fought the opponent who defeated you."

So the first step is to help our kids recognize the fears that have become so wrapped around their personalities that they don't even acknowledge them anymore. Unless they face them squarely, they will punch vaguely at the air, trying to fight what they sense is there—but since they have no idea what they are, they're just wasting energy.

But how do we help them do that? How do we help them pull up the roots of fear that have so firmly embedded themselves in their hearts and minds?

This book is about pulling up those roots. For many children, the roots are so deep they have no idea how to begin untangling them from their daily thoughts. So, taking 40 days to uproot this muddle is reasonable.

Therefore, you need to help your children pull up roots, but you also need to help them become intimately aware of who God is and what he wants to do in their lives. Only as they learn to give fears to a God who loves and cares for them will they have freedom from the anxieties that plague them.

Over 40 days, you can take a closer look at any misconceptions your child has had about God and face the fact that they've been trying to take his job, living under the illusion they can actually master their fears and worries on their own.

Corrie ten Boom, a woman whose writings have had a profound effect in my life, said, "Worrying is carrying tomorrow's load with today's strength—carrying two days at once. It is moving into tomorrow ahead of time. Worrying doesn't empty tomorrow of its sorrow, it empties today of its strength." She was able to say this in spite of being interned in the Nazi concentration camp where her sister died.

That's the kind of confidence in God we want our kids to have—so unshakeable that it can carry them through the worst life can throw at them. It would be wonderful if we could help our children understand the dichotomy of Frederick Buechner's wisdom in his book *Beyond Words*: "Here is the world. Beautiful and terrible things will happen. Don't be afraid."

Preparation for the 40-Day Journey

My granddaughter inherited my good imagination. When she was three years old, she was afraid of everything. She feared that wild animals lurked in the dining room when the lights were off, that the next page in the storybook was going to show a cat scratching a dog (we skipped that page), and that any food other than peanut butter would poison her.

Of course, we know those fears are ridiculous. Most of us go through life never worrying about carnivores in the house, are able to read about interactions between animal species without batting an eye, and eat a wide variety of foods. But looking at her fears has made me wonder what our fears look like to God. Are our fears just as silly to him? Does he take our immaturity into account just as I do with my granddaughter?

Such fears remind me of Leviticus 26:36: "You will live in such fear that the sound of a leaf driven by the wind will send you fleeing. You will run as though fleeing from a sword, and you will fall even when no one pursues you" (NLT).

That verse describes the fear I lived with for years. Nevertheless, fear is a universal human emotion. David says in Psalm 55:4–6, "My heart pounds in my chest. . . . Fear and trembling overwhelm me, and I can't stop shaking. Oh, that I had wings like a dove, then I would fly away and rest" (NLT).

Have you felt that way at times? Felt fear so palpable that it affected you physically, and you wanted simply to flee?

Yet there are valid things to fear: loss of a job, possessions, health, family, and even life. So how can we deal with our natural fear?

David goes on to say in Psalm 55:16–18, "But I will call on God, and the LORD will rescue me. Morning, noon, and night I cry out in my distress, and the LORD hears my voice. He ransoms me and keeps me safe from the battle waged against me" (NLT).

Note that battle waged against David. God didn't stop the battle—it still roared on around him. God doesn't always change our circumstances. We may pray that he heal our cancer, deliver us from bankruptcy, or protect us from harm during war, but he doesn't always do that.

However, children are not emotionally equipped to deal with fears the way adults do. So we must teach them wise caution without frightening them in the process. Warn them not to go anywhere with strangers, but don't terrify them with all the gory details that might happen to them if they do. At this point in their lives, children need you to handle the scary details of life. They put their confidence in you, and you have to carry that for them.

But we can teach our children to respond as David did, crying out to God all day for help with our fears. Children need to know they can trust God and his never-failing love and character, even if God doesn't change their circumstances. David goes on to say in Psalm 55:22, "Give your burdens to the LORD, and he will take care of you. He will not permit the godly to slip and fall" (NLT). Though David's words seem contradictory, the truth is that even when we do slip and fall, God is still faithful to us. We can trust his care, even when that care doesn't deliver us from our difficulties. This is what our children need to understand.

We must teach our kids that they have a choice about how to handle their fear. They can let it paralyze them, or they can surrender what they cannot control to God and decide to move forward in faith—camping on the certainty that no matter what happens, God loves them. In Romans 8:38, the apostle Paul writes, "I am convinced that nothing can ever separate us from God's love. Neither death nor life, neither angels nor demons, neither our fears for today nor our worries about tomorrow—not even the powers of hell can separate us from God's love" (NLT).

Nothing could be better than a good, wise Father who loves us so much that he's working way beyond our understanding to bring us the best—he's behind the scenes working on our behalf, even in the midst of our fears. If that's the case, then we really do have nothing to fear. This is the certainty we want our children to absorb and live.

How to Proceed

Therefore, the way to help our children out of fear is to assist them in rooting themselves firmly in who God is. By understanding his character, they can learn to trust him with the daily details of their lives.

That's why this book takes 40 days to examine God's attributes. As your kids gain insight into who he is, they will be flooded with the truth that he cares for them and intends good for them, and this takes the place of the lies that their imaginations conjure up.

I highly recommend that once you start this book with your kids, you take it seriously enough to complete it. Set aside the entire 40 days and don't give up until you've seen it through.

Also, although you can make great strides in helping your kids overcome their fears, they will still have to deal with anxiety if that's part of their personality. I am an anxious person and am convinced that is something I will have to submit to Christ over and over again. I no longer am bound by constant imaginary fears, but I still feel anxiety regularly. I feel anxious when I have to meet new people, be in charge of an event, meet a deadline, or counsel someone in distress. Your kids may have such lingering anxieties as well, but hopefully after 40 days, they will have some lifelong tools to deal with that anxiety.

Here are some other things that may help your children as you set aside these 40 days:

1. **Keep the communication lines open with your kids.** You could just give this book to your child and ask them to read through it, but you would be missing a great opportunity to discuss what your kids are really fearing. Over 40 days you could foster a close relationship with your child, which will do more than anything in helping them manage their fears.

2. **Don't belittle or make fun of their fears, no matter how petty they seem to you.** As I mentioned earlier, the fears that kids

have can seem pretty silly until we think about our own fears. The more we can relate to their fears, the more kids will trust us and believe that we understand. And if they believe you understand them, they will more easily believe that God loves and understands them.

3. **Share your own battles and victories over fear and worry.** The more you can tell your kids about your own struggles and mastery of those battles, the more hope you give them that help is possible for them too. Be honest and don't whitewash the ways God has moved you past your own fears.

Along with letting go of fears, you will want to help your children embrace God's many blessings. Over the 40 days, ask him to open your children's eyes to his goodness so they can soak it all in. Children need to see that God's grace is amazing, and that we don't deserve anything he gives us. Every blessing and victory we experience are by his goodness. Kids will see that an attitude of praise and thankfulness can turn everything around, because they will begin to see God working everywhere in their lives and circumstances.

I pray these 40 days will usher your child into a new phase of enjoying God. Instead of constantly worrying, your child can learn to just enjoy being in God's presence. They can learn at an early age to listen for his voice and delight in what he has made them for and called them to do.

How This Book Is Organized

Each day of the 40-day journey starts with a Scripture passage, a short meditation on that passage, a few questions, and a prayer.

If you do it in the morning, it might help to mention the devotional again at the end of the day to remind your child that they can sleep soundly knowing of God's love and care for them. Many children have anxieties about bedtime, and this can help them manage those.

Also, if your child is discouraged that they didn't do well that day managing their fears, don't make them feel guilty about that. That's why there are 40 days to this journey! They have plenty more days to practice giving their fears to God.

Finally, I would like to add that if your child has a clinically diagnosed anxiety disorder, this method may or may not work for them. There could be other, more complex things at play. Regardless, it will be useful for your child to immerse himself in learning who God is and to work through some of the things that cause him anxiety.

Day 1: Who Is God?
Loving

Scripture Reading

Your unfailing love, O LORD, is as vast as the heavens;
  your faithfulness reaches beyond the clouds.
Your righteousness is like the mighty mountains,
  your justice like the ocean depths.
You care for people and animals alike, O LORD.
  How precious is your unfailing love, O God!
All humanity finds shelter
  in the shadow of your wings.
You feed them from the abundance of your own house,
  letting them drink from your river of delights.
For you are the fountain of life,
  the light by which we see. (Ps. 36:5–9, NLT)

Emma loved to be with her mom at night. They would often work on homework together and then talk about how things went at school that day. She could tell her mom all the things that happened and know her mom would always be on her side.

But when it got closer to bedtime, Emma would start to worry. She didn't like being in a dark room by herself. In her room, she couldn't see her mom, who made her feel safe, so she would begin to feel afraid and imagine all sorts of bad things.

So, Emma told her mom that the reason she often doesn't want to go to bed is because she hates the dark and is afraid of it. Her mom read the verses above and assured her that as much as she loved her, she couldn't be with her all the time, but that Jesus could always be with her. She could go to sleep knowing he would always love her and care for her. Emma decided to go to sleep imagining that Jesus was there holding her hand, and it made her feel loved and cared for.

⇒ Are you afraid of the dark? If so, what are you most afraid of when the lights are off?
⇒ How can knowing Jesus loves you help you be less afraid at night?

Prayer

Jesus, thank you that you love me more than anyone else ever can. And thank you that you want to take care of me, even when others can't be with me every minute. Hold my hand as I fall asleep tonight, Jesus, and take care of me all night long.

Day 2: Who Is God?
Faithful

Scripture Reading

He is the Rock; his deeds are perfect.
   Everything he does is just and fair.
He is a faithful God who does no wrong;
   how just and upright he is! (Deut. 32:4, NLT)

Caden felt nervous about going to school. His family had moved over the summer and so the school was new, the teacher was new, and he didn't really have any friends yet.

The first day of school was okay, but he was lonely. He didn't really have anyone to play with on the playground. The second day felt the same way. But on the third day, Mason noticed a bigger boy was picking on Caden. The boy wasn't hurting Caden, but Mason could see that the big boy was talking in a mean way. Mason was trying to decide what to do when the bigger boy gave Caden a little shove and walked away from him.

Mason ran over to Caden and asked if he was okay. When Caden told him he was, Mason said, "That boy is mean to everyone. Just stay away from him. Do you want to go play kick ball with me and the other boys?"

Caden was delighted and found a good friend in Mason. After that Mason looked for him every day and they became fast friends. So, when Caden heard that God is faithful, he thought of Mason. But God is even more faithful than Mason. There are times that Mason let Caden down, even when he didn't mean to. And there were times that Mason just couldn't be around when Caden needed him. But God would always be there with him, so he didn't ever need to be afraid.

⟹ What do you think it means to be faithful?
⟹ How is God even more faithful than a person can be?

Prayer

I put myself in your care, Lord. I believe you are faithful and that you will be with me and take care of me, no matter what I face. When I am scared, help me to remember that.

Day 3: Who Is God?
Joyful

Scripture Reading

Send out your light and your truth;
  let them guide me.
Let them lead me to your holy mountain,
  to the place where you live.
There I will go to the altar of God,
  to God—the source of all my joy.
I will praise you with my harp,
  O God, my God!
Why am I discouraged?
  Why is my heart so sad?
I will put my hope in God!
  I will praise him again—
  my Savior and my God! (Ps. 43:3-5, NLT)

Lillian loved to play with Karsten. Each time she was around him, he made her laugh. He even made her laugh when she was feeling upset about something.

For example, one day she had woken up feeling upset. She hadn't slept well and when her mom woke her up for school, she couldn't quite get going. They were also out of her favorite cereal, so she had to eat toast instead. And then when she left the house, it was raining—and the bus was late, so she got soaked as she waited. She began to feel afraid and anxious about the day. She just knew it was going to be one bad thing after another.

But when she got to school, she saw Karsten. He told her a joke and made her smile for the first time that day. She felt things begin to get better from then on.

Our psalm today says that God is the "source of all my joy." We often think of joy as a time when we are happy and everything is going our way, but it's much more than that. Just as Karsten helped turn Lillian's day around, that's what thinking about God does for us. He invented joy and we find that joy when we think about how wonderful he is instead of how unhappy we are. God is waiting for us to come to him so we don't have to feel anxious and worried, but instead think about how he wants us to be joyful in him instead of worried about the things that go wrong.

⇒ What do you think it means to be joyful?
⇒ Why is that more than just having things go our way?
⇒ How can God make us more joyful than people can?

Prayer

Lord, it is so easy for me to pretend that things are okay when they are not. I can tell myself things are no big deal, but then I know that's not true. Help me to recognize when I am just pretending not to feel anxious. Help me to see why I am feeling anxious and to deal with it head on instead of pretending I don't feel overwhelmed. After I identify my fear, help me to run to you, the source of all my joy.

Day 4: Who Is God?
Kind

Scripture Reading

Please, Lord, remember,
  you have always
  been patient and kind.
Forget each wrong I did
  when I was young.
  Show how truly kind you are
  and remember me.
You are honest and merciful,
  and you teach sinners
  how to follow your path.
You lead humble people
  to do what is right
  and to stay on your path.
In everything you do,
  you are kind and faithful
  to everyone who keeps
  our agreement with you.
Be true to your name, Lord,
  by forgiving each one
  of my terrible sins.
You will show the right path
  to all who worship you.
They will have plenty,
  and then their children
  will receive the land. (Ps. 25:6–13, CEV)

According to the *Cambridge Dictionary*, to be kind means to be "generous, helpful, and caring about other people." When Janna heard that definition, she thought of her grandma. Just last week, Janna had told her grandma about how a friend of hers made fun of the way she had dressed. It hurt her feelings and Janna didn't know how to get over it. Her grandma listened to how Janna felt and reassured her that God loved her no matter how she looked. And she also told her a story of how someone had made fun of her when she was a kid. It made Janna feel she wasn't so alone. It also made her think about how Jesus went through far worse from other people when he was on earth. Somehow that comforted her, knowing that Jesus understood what it felt like to have others not understand.

Janna's grandma told her that we fail to see God's kindness when we don't get something we want. She said, "If we instead dwell on all the ways God has cared for us even when we have been unfaithful and disobedient, we are bowled over by his kindness to us. And that can help even when people are mean to us."

She went on to say, "Keeping God's kindness in mind is tremendously helpful as I deal with my fear. A lot of my fear stems from the fact that I believe God *can* keep me and those I love safe, but I'm not sure he *will* do so. When I am troubled with those kinds of doubts and fears, I need to remember God's intention toward me is to always be kind. No matter what I am going through, his kindness is central to my future. He will *always* act out of that kindness and will never fail to do so in any way."

The next day when Janna saw the friend who had made fun of her, she felt afraid and didn't want to be around her. But then she thought of how God wants to be kind to her *and* to her friend. She remembered the words from the psalm: "you have always been patient and kind" and it gave her courage to smile and talk to her friend.

⇒ Ask your mom or dad to tell you about a time that someone was unkind to them. How did they handle that?

⇒ How can remembering that God is *always* patient and kind help you when others are not?

⇒ How can knowing this help you get over your fears of other people who are unkind?

Prayer

Lord, help me to understand that you long to show me kindness, but that I am often too bound up in my fears and anxiety to recognize it. Open my eyes to your kindness today. Help me to notice it in the big things and the small things. Even when things don't go my way, help me to know you are always kind. Help me to recognize that you have always been patient and kind and that nothing will ever change that.

Day 5: Who Is God?
Gentle

Scripture Reading

Then Jesus said, "I thank you, Father, Lord of heaven and earth. I praise you because you have hidden these things from the people who are wise and smart. But you have shown them to those who are like little children. Yes, Father, this is what you really wanted.

"My Father has given me all things. No one knows the Son—only the Father knows the Son. And no one knows the Father—only the Son knows the Father. And the only people who will know about the Father are those whom the Son chooses to tell.

"Come to me, all of you who are tired and have heavy loads. I will give you rest. Accept my work and learn from me. I am gentle and humble in spirit. And you will find rest for your souls. The work that I ask you to accept is easy. The load I give you to carry is not heavy." (Matt. 11:25–30, ICB)

Marcus was afraid of God. He thought of him as big, powerful, and kind of mean. A teacher had once told him that God expected a lot of him and that he'd better live up to God's standards, or he would be sorry. That left him afraid that God was always waiting for him to mess up.

But when his dad read this passage to him, he began to think another way. Jesus was talking about God differently from how Marcus usually feels about him. First he said that God shows himself to those who are like little children. That gave him hope that God cared about him for merely being a child and thinking like a child.

He also pictured Jesus throwing his arms open wide as he invited everyone who is tired and has a heavy load to come to him. That sounded like someone very gentle, not someone mean who was waiting to catch him making a mistake.

Those verses changed the way Marcus thought about God. His fear of God felt like a heavy load that he was finally able to set down. His fear of God had felt like a runaway horse that was dragging him through the mud. That day, he told Jesus he wanted to trade that runaway horse for him.

⇒ Do you think of God as gentle? Why or why not?
⇒ Are you afraid that God will be mean to you if you make a mistake? Why is that not true?
⇒ Everyone does the wrong thing now and then. Ask your mom or dad a time they did something wrong and how they still know God loves them.

Prayer

Jesus, I know you are humble and gentle. That is part of what draws me to you. You long to take my heavy load. I ask you to remind me of this throughout the day. As I feel the weight of my fears, I pray that you'll remind me that you'll gently lift the heavy load from my shoulders and carry it for me.

Day 6: Who Is God?
Ever-present

Scripture Reading

O Lord, you have examined my heart
  and know everything about me.
You know when I sit down or stand up.
  You know my thoughts even when I'm far away.
You see me when I travel
  and when I rest at home.
  You know everything I do.
You know what I am going to say
  even before I say it, Lord.
You go before me and follow me.
  You place your hand of blessing on my head.
Such knowledge is too wonderful for me,
  too great for me to understand!
I can never escape from your Spirit!
  I can never get away from your presence!
If I go up to heaven, you are there;
  if I go down to the grave, you are there.
If I ride the wings of the morning,
  if I dwell by the farthest oceans,
even there your hand will guide me,
  and your strength will support me.
I could ask the darkness to hide me
  and the light around me to become night—
  but even in darkness I cannot hide from you.
To you the night shines as bright as day.

Darkness and light are the same to you. (Ps. 139:1–12, NLT)

Sonya felt alone a lot. She lived in the country and didn't have friends nearby. She had a little brother, but he was a lot younger than her and didn't like to do the kind of things she liked to do. So many days after school, she spent the day by herself in her room. And at night, when the lights went out, she felt very alone. She knew she was too old to be scared of the dark anymore, but she was. She just wished someone was with her when she was afraid.

One of those nights when she was afraid, she read this psalm. The beginning rattled her because she realized she can't put anything over on God. Although she may fool others, God knows everything she is thinking. But in spite of that, this psalm reassures her that God loves her and wants to enter into her thoughts—even when they are bad thoughts. As the psalmist says, "You go before me and follow me. You place your hand of blessing on my head. Such knowledge is too wonderful for me, too great for me to understand!"

So even though God knows all her thoughts, he places his hand of blessing on her head. As Sonya read this she said, "You follow me, you surround me, and you keep your hand on me. I can hardly believe this! It's more than I can take in! You never, ever let go of me, even when I mess up."

She thought of the way her mother took care of her when she was a very young child, keeping a firm hand on her to keep her safe, stroking her head to help her get to sleep at night, doing everything possible to make sure she was loved and cared for. She thought of her little brother, who was still learning to behave. Even when he was mean to her mom, even when he was completely unlikeable, Sonya knew her mom still loved him, even if he got into trouble.

It helped Sonya to think that whether she traveled or rested at home, God is there. And he's a loving God who cares about her and wants to carry her through her toughest times.

So what does this mean for her fears? She is never alone! He will never leave her for a moment. As she tried to go to sleep, she found this especially comforting as she felt alone and afraid. Her imagination can conjure up all sorts of disasters, but she instead imagined that Jesus is right beside her, because he is!

Of all the words in the psalm, Sonya most liked the phrase "To you the night shines as bright as day." She thought about that as she drifted to sleep peacefully, knowing God saw everything, even in the dark, and that meant she didn't have to be afraid of anything.

⇒ Is it hard for you to be alone at night? Why?

⇒ What words in this psalm help you the most? Why?

⇒ How can you learn to imagine Jesus with you instead of all the other scary things you might imagine?

Prayer

Lord, help me to picture you at my side, protecting me every moment. I ask that when I am fearful you'll remind me you have promised, "I will never fail you. I will never abandon you" (Heb. 13:5, NLT). When I feel scared, help me to be aware that you are with me and want to care for me.

Day 7: Who Is God?
Peaceful

Scripture Reading

Be full of joy in the Lord always. I will say again, be full of joy.

Let all men see that you are gentle and kind. The Lord is coming soon. Do not worry about anything. But pray and ask God for everything you need. And when you pray, always give thanks. And God's peace will keep your hearts and minds in Christ Jesus. The peace that God gives is so great that we cannot understand it. (Phil. 4:4–7, ICB)

Andrew worried about everything. He worried that he would be late for school, that he would get in trouble while he was there, that his friends would be mean to him, that his teacher would be disappointed with him, and that he'd get a low grade on his upcoming test.

So when he read this passage in Philippians, he was surprised that it said not to worry about anything! How was he supposed to that? There were so many things to worry about.

He began to think about the first verse that talks about being full of joy. He was pretty sure he was not. He was too full of worries for any joy to get through. Having joy didn't feel possible. And how in the world was he supposed to get it?

Maybe he just had to ask. That's what this passage says: ask God for everything you need. And when you pray, always give thanks.

He decided to try it the next day. When he woke up and started being afraid he was going to be late to school, he prayed, "Jesus, help me not to be afraid. Just take that away. Thank you."

Then when he got to school, he saw one of his friends. He started to feel afraid he might lose that friend, so he prayed, "Jesus, help me to not be afraid of losing my friend, James. Help me to just enjoy him. Thank you."

When the teacher passed out a test, Andrew felt afraid he would not do well, so he prayed, "Jesus, help me to not be afraid and to just do my best. I know you love me know matter how I do on this test. Thank you."

By the end of the day, Andrew not only didn't feel afraid, but he felt peaceful.

⇒ When you start each day, what are some of the things you feel afraid of?
⇒ Why do those things make you afraid?
⇒ How might praying about each of those things as Andrew did help you?

Prayer

Father, help me to know and deeply understand that you are peace. That means if I am feeling anxious about my day, that worry is not from you. It is just my imagination making me think things are going to be bad. Help me to remember to pray about the things that worry me and to thank you for the help you promise to give. No matter what happens today, help me to know that you are with me and intend good for me. Fill me with your peace, which I can only understand with your help.

Day 8: Who Is God?
Patient

Scripture Reading

I thank Christ Jesus our Lord because he trusted me and gave me this work of serving him. And he gives me strength. In the past I spoke against Christ and persecuted him and did all kinds of things to hurt him. But God showed mercy to me because I did not know what I was doing. I did those things when I did not believe. But the grace of our Lord was fully given to me. And with that grace came the faith and love that are in Christ Jesus.

What I say is true, and you should fully accept it: Christ Jesus came into the world to save sinners. And I am the worst of those sinners. But I was given mercy. I was given mercy so that in me Christ Jesus could show that he has patience without limit. And he showed his patience with me, the worst of all sinners. Christ wanted me to be an example for those who would believe in him and have life forever. Honor and glory to the King that rules forever! He cannot be destroyed and cannot be seen. Honor and glory forever and ever to the only God. Amen. (1 Tim. 1:12–17, ICB)

Paul is writing to Timothy in this passage. We think of Paul as a great hero of the faith, but in these verses, he is telling us everything he did wrong. He was against Christ and against Christians and calls himself the worst of sinners. But God had mercy on him and had now appointed him to do his work. The wonder of that never leaves Paul. He writes about it in several of his letters—evidently amazed that God would not only forgive him but give him a job to do.

I don't know what you've done wrong, but it's unlikely that

whatever it was is worse than what Paul did. He said bad things about Christ at every turn and was determined to wipe out all of Jesus' followers. And yet God was patient with him. He allowed him to blunder on in his misguided way until the exact right moment when Jesus confronted him and gave him a new task. This affected Paul so much that he begins most of his letters by talking about the God of mercy and grace, even as he goes on to correct the churches in what they are doing wrong.

What does that have to do with our fears? If your fears have anything to do with how you've failed and fear failing again, this passage should give you great courage. God is patient. This is obvious not only from the New Testament but from the Old Testament as well. God was patient with Israel for centuries, even though they turned their back on him. His patience is not endless, and we should never think we can thumb our nose at him, but if we sincerely want to follow him he is remarkably patient with our failures.

As you go through your day, ask God to show you the ways that you fear failing. And when he does, ask him to help you have victory over your fears. Memorize the phrase "God showed mercy to me," and say it to yourself when you feel you've messed up once again.

⇒ How do you feel when you know you've done something wrong?
⇒ What does it mean that God wants to show you mercy? (Ask one of your parents what that means if you are having trouble figuring it out.)
⇒ How can you remind yourself of how patient God is?

Prayer

Dear, patient God, help me to see you as you are. Help me to see your great patience with me and that you understand I make mistakes and do things wrong at times. I want to learn to trust you, so help me to remember how patient you are with me today so I can be braver than I ever thought possible.

Day 9: Who Is God?
Good

Scripture Reading

O Lord, you are so good, so ready to forgive,
   so full of unfailing love for all who ask for your help.
Listen closely to my prayer, O Lord;
   hear my urgent cry.
I will call to you whenever I'm in trouble,
   and you will answer me. (Ps. 86:5–7, NLT)

Olivia went to Ginny's house for the first time. She didn't know Ginny very well, but her parents had to go away and Ginny's family offered to take care of her for the weekend. Olivia was afraid because she knew she would miss her mom and her home. No one else understood everything about her and what she liked and didn't like. That made going to a new place scary for her.

Olivia felt nervous all through dinner. The more she thought about the weekend, the worse she felt. She didn't like the food they served and had trouble swallowing it, because it wasn't the way her parents made food at home. But after dinner, Ginny's dad read the psalm above. When he finished, he said, "The Psalms help us understand what God is like. David wrote this one as a prayer, calling out to God and feeling certain that he would answer him when he was in trouble. He also says early in the psalm that God is good and forgiving. Knowing that helped him trust God with the difficult things in his life. Because he knew God is good, he could ask him for help and know he would give it."

Olivia thought about that. She wondered if she really believed that

God is good. Because if she did, she would know he wants what is best for her. She decided to ask Ginny's dad a question.

"If I am afraid or worried about something, does that mean I don't really think God is good?"

Ginny's dad seemed glad she asked this question. "In a way. Of course, we are all afraid or worried at times, but if we stay there and build up those fears, they become worse and worse. Then we do not really believe God loves us. But if we ask God for help with our fears, it shows we really believe that he loves us. That must make him very happy."

Olivia thought about this as she drifted to sleep that night. She told God how afraid she was of the weekend, but that she truly did believe he loved her. "So, God, help me to know you are with me this weekend, even if I do miss my parents and home."

Olivia slept well that night. She still had moments of fear and worry that weekend, and she still didn't like the food, but she knew God loved her and was with her. That was enough.

⇒ How does believing God is good help take away our fears?
⇒ If God is good, what does that mean about even the bad things that happen to me?

Prayer

Heavenly Father, help me to know that you are truly good. I know you are better than anyone I have ever known. Help me to always be certain that you are good and that what you do in my life is good too, even if I don't always like it. Help me to always ask for your help when I'm afraid.

Day 10: Who Is God?
Ruler of All

Scripture Reading

God . . . is the blessed and only Ruler. He is the King of all kings and the Lord of all lords. God is the only One who never dies. He lives in light so bright that men cannot go near it. No one has ever seen God, or can see him. May honor and power belong to God forever. Amen. (1 Tim. 6:15–16, ICB)

Lucas thought the words *ruler* and *king* were very old words. He didn't think anyone really lived under a king's rule anymore. It sounded like the stories he read about long ago, but no one lived under a king's rules now, did they? It sounded like a bad idea, because all those old kings he read about often did a bad job. That's why nations like the United States of America came to be, to get away from kings.

But in this passage, Paul says to Timothy that God is the only Ruler and that he is the "King of all kings and Lord of all lords." He lives in light so bright that people can't go near it. That must be why none of us has ever seen God. But even though we don't see him, he is in charge of everything. And the Bible says that's a good thing.

Lucas wondered, *So if God rules over everything, what does that mean for my fears?* He thought about that a long time because he was afraid of his new teacher. She was very strict, and since she was in charge all day long, Lucas felt afraid of what she might do if he did something wrong.

He decided that he couldn't do anything about his teacher, but it helped him to think that God was even more in charge than she was. Somehow that made it easier to go to school. He knew that God was in charge of everything, and that meant that he didn't have to be afraid.

He also thought about the old kings from long ago that he'd read about. They seemed very powerful to those who lived in their kingdoms, but in the end they just died and someone took their place. Lucas thought, *That will never happen to God. He will always be in charge.*

That would be scary if Marcus didn't believe the things he'd already learned about God. Because he knew God is loving, faithful, joyful, kind, gentle, ever present, peaceful, patient, and good, he knew he could trust him with his fear of his teacher.

⇒ Is there someone in charge that you are afraid of? If so, why?
⇒ How does it help to know that God is in charge of that person who is in charge of you?

Prayer

King of all kings and Lord of all lords, you are the only One who never dies. You live in light so bright that we can't go near it. You are the only one who rules over everything and everyone. May honor and power belong to you forever. Amen.

Day 11: Who Is God?
Father

Scripture Reading

Grace and peace to you from God our Father and the Lord Jesus Christ. Praise be to the God and Father of our Lord Jesus Christ. God is the Father who is full of mercy. And he is the God of all comfort. He comforts us every time we have trouble, so that we can comfort others when they have trouble. We can comfort them with the same comfort that God gives us. (2 Cor. 1:2–4, ICB)

Janna didn't know her father. He had left the family when she was very young and never visited, so she only had a few pictures to even know what he looked like. So, when her mom read the verses above that talked about God being a father, she liked it.

She asked her mom more about the kind of father God is. Her mom said, "He's the kind of Father it talks about in Matthew 6:26: Look at the birds. They don't plant or harvest or store food in barns, for your heavenly Father feeds them. And aren't you far more valuable to him than they are? (NLT).

"Or listen to this verse: So if you sinful people know how to give good gifts to your children, how much more will your heavenly Father give good gifts to those who ask him (Matt. 7:11, NLT).

"So he is the kind of Father who wants to take care of his children. He has taken care of us ever since your dad left. He's the best father possible."

Janna said, "But I'd still like to have a father like everyone else."

"Of course you do," her mother answered, "but whether that happens or not, you can know that God is a more generous father than any man on earth can be. And when you are afraid, keep in mind that God wants to care for you and comfort you. Just ask for his help, and he will give it."

⇒ Why is God the best possible father?
⇒ When you are afraid, how can knowing that help you?
⇒ Is there something you want to ask his help for right now?

Prayer
Dear Father who loves me, help me to know how much you care about me. Let me know your kindness and see your moment-by-moment care for me. Help me to trust you fully with my fears. Amen.

Day 12: Who Is God?
Brother

Scripture Reading

Jesus, who makes people holy, and those who are made holy are from the same family. So he is not ashamed to call them his brothers. He says . . ."I am here. And with me are the children that God has given me."

These children are people with physical bodies. So Jesus himself became like them and had the same experiences they have . . . And now he can help those who are tempted. He is able to help because he himself suffered and was tempted. (Heb. 2:11–18, ICB)

Jackson liked that verse. He didn't have any brothers, so it was great to think that Jesus was his brother. His friend Aiden had an older brother who was pretty mean to him, and he knew Jesus was the kind of brother who would always look out for him and never be mean to him.

So, not only was God his father, but Christ was his brother. Jackson knew he was the perfect older brother who would never pick on him, but instead would help him when he was having a hard time or being tempted.

Jackson thought about that at school because he was afraid of Aiden's big brother, Carter. So when school let out and Carter started to pick on him, Jackson thought about how Jesus went through all kinds of suffering when he was on earth. That helped him to shrug off Carter's comments that usually hurt his feelings and made him feel bad. He thought, *I have a big brother so much better than the kind of brother you are to Aiden. He understands me and cares for me.*

Then a few days later, Jackson was spending time with Aiden at his house. Aiden wanted him to watch a movie that he knew his mom wouldn't approve of. Jackson thought of Jesus who was his brother, and knew Jesus would encourage him to not do something wrong just because his friend wanted him to. So, Jackson told Aiden he'd rather play and game, which Aiden was happy to do.

⇒ What does it mean to you that Jesus is your brother?
⇒ How might that help you when you are afraid of something or someone?
⇒ How might that help you when you are tempted to do something wrong?

Prayer

Jesus, thank you for becoming a human being and making me part of your family. I love that you want to be my brother. That means you understand what my life is like and want to help me. When I am afraid, help me to remember you are with me.

Day 13: Who Is God?
Trustworthy

Scripture Reading

God wanted to prove that his promise was true. He wanted to prove this to those who would get what he promised. He wanted them to understand clearly that his purposes never change. So God proved his promise by also making an oath. These two things cannot change. God cannot lie when he makes a promise, and he cannot lie when he makes an oath. These things encourage us who came to God for safety. They give us strength to hold on to the hope we have been given. We have this hope as an anchor for the soul, sure and strong. It enters behind the curtain in the Most Holy Place in heaven. (Heb. 6:17–19, ICB)

Ava was going to a week-long camp for the first time. She felt safe when she was at home, so going to camp sounded scary. She wasn't sure how she would do away from her family. The whole idea made her nervous. But she had signed up to go, and her parents said she had to carry through with it.

Right before she got into the car to go to camp, her mom read the verses we read today. The part that stuck in her mind was that Jesus would be the anchor for her soul. She liked that phrase, and it would be easy to think about at camp since there was a lake with boats there.

On the second day of camp, Ava felt very homesick. She was afraid she wouldn't make it through the whole week without crying. Then she looked at the lake and thought how Jesus was her anchor. He was with her! Even if she missed her family, Jesus was with her and he would never leave her. She was so glad she could trust Jesus that her feelings changed immediately. Her counselor had been watching her and noticed that she had looked as though she was going to cry, but now she was smiling.

> ⇒ Have you ever felt as Ava did? Afraid of being away from family and friends? Tell me about it.
> ⇒ What does it mean that you can trust Jesus, even when you are lonely or afraid?

Prayer

Jesus, you are truly my refuge and the anchor of my soul. Thank you for your constant presence and steadfast faithfulness to me when I need you most. Help me to know you are with me and that I am safe under your care.

Day 14: Who Is God?
Wise

Scripture Reading

"He said to his brothers, "I am Joseph. Is my father still alive?" But the brothers could not answer him, because they were very afraid of him. So Joseph said to them, "Come close to me." So the brothers came close to him. And he said to them, "I am your brother Joseph. You sold me as a slave to go to Egypt. Now don't be worried. Don't be angry with yourselves because you sold me here. God sent me here ahead of you to save people's lives. No food has grown on the land for two years now. And there will be five more years without planting or harvest. So God sent me here ahead of you. This was to make sure you have some descendants left on earth. And it was to keep you alive in an amazing way. So it was not you who sent me here, but God. God has made me the highest officer of the king of Egypt. I am in charge of his palace. I am the master of all the land of Egypt." (Gen. 45:3–8, ICB)

We can learn a great deal from Joseph about how to handle fear. This is the Joseph who was sold into slavery by his brothers and who was thrown into prison when he didn't even do anything wrong. In this scene, he tells his brothers who he is, and as he does, we see how wise God is.

Surely, when Joseph was first making that long journey to Egypt, or when he was sitting in prison, ignored by the one who promised to help get him out, he must have felt great fear. I have no doubt that at times it was overwhelming and all-consuming. He probably even felt abandoned by God, and certainly must have wondered what in the world God was doing. But by this scene, he had worked through all that.

Looking back, he recognized that God had a plan all along and was allowing Joseph to go through each step of this journey for a reason.

So what does that mean for us and for our fears? It means that if we are seeking God, he is working—even when it seems to make no sense. Because of Joseph's example and confidence in God's wisdom, we can have the same certainty that God is working in and through us. As a result, we can let our fears drift away as we remain rooted in God's wisdom. We can echo Paul's words in Romans 16:27: "All glory to the only wise God, through Jesus Christ, forever. Amen." (NLT)

Today as you face your fears, let that description of God drive those fears away. The "only wise God" has not abandoned you and is working to accomplish good in and through you.

⇒ How do you think Joseph had such a good attitude when things went so terribly wrong at first?
⇒ How can you trust that God is wise and knows what he is doing, even when things seem to be going wrong? Give an example.

Prayer

You are truly the only wise God and the only one who can see the big picture. Help me to trust you with the details of my life that often do not make sense to me. Take away my fears as I lean heavily on you and depend on you to turn confusion into certainty. Amen.

Day 15: Who Is God?
Self-Sufficient

Scripture Passage

Paul . . . said, "Men of Athens, I can see that you are very religious in all things. I was going through your city, and I saw the things you worship. I found an altar that had these words written on it: "TO A GOD WHO IS NOT KNOWN." You worship a god that you don't know. This is the God I am telling you about! He is the God who made the whole world and everything in it. He is the Lord of the land and the sky. He does not live in temples that men build! This God is the One who gives life, breath, and everything else to people. He does not need any help from them. He has everything he needs. God began by making one man. From him came all the different people who live everywhere in the world. He decided exactly when and where they must live. (Acts 17:22–26, ICB)

When Noah invited Oliver over to his house for dinner, Oliver was glad to go. He liked the way Noah was kind to the other kids and stood up for those who couldn't stand up for themselves.

At dinner, Noah's father read the verse from the Bible we just read and prayed for their meal. Oliver had never been in a church before. He'd never heard anyone pray aloud or heard anything read from the Bible. This was so new to him that he didn't know what he was supposed to do or how to respond. So, when they began eating, Oliver said, "That scares me that you talk to God. I don't know much about God, so the idea of talking to him frightens me."

Noah's father listened to Oliver and said, "As our verses said, 'God is the One who gives life, breath, and everything else to people. He does not need any help from them. He has everything he needs.' So, God doesn't need anyone to do anything for him and has no unmet needs. He never fails to be in control. There is nothing he lacks and no purpose he cannot accomplish. Perhaps the best way to understand what it means that God is self-sufficient is by considering the opposite: God will never be helpless, poor, hopeless, lack anything, powerless, or weak.

"But that especially means that you don't have to be afraid of him. As it says in Romans 8:31, 'If God is for us, who can be against us?' If he is truly self-sufficient, nothing is beyond him. Our worries for safety, food, clothing, courage, health, friendship, and so on go away as we trust each of those things to a God who can do anything."

Oliver went home with a lot to think about. He would have many more conversations with Noah and Noah's dad about what God is like, and the more he learned, the less afraid he was of him.

⇒ Do you have a friend who doesn't know anything about God? If so, how might you begin to talk to that friend about God?
⇒ Since God will never be helpless, poor, hopeless, lack anything, powerless, or weak, what does that mean for the things you are afraid of? Think about each thing and how it helps you overcome your fears.

Prayer
Lord, you truly are a God who doesn't need anything. As I face all the needs, fears, and worries of my day, I pray you will help me keep that in mind and to trust you to help me with all the things that bother me.

Day 16: Who Is God?
All-Knowing

Scripture Reading

O Lord, you have examined my heart
and know everything about me.
You know when I sit down or stand up.
You know my thoughts even when I'm far away.
You see me when I travel
and when I rest at home.
You know everything I do.
You know what I am going to say
even before I say it, Lord.
You go before me and follow me.
You place your hand of blessing on my head.
Such knowledge is too wonderful for me,
too great for me to understand! (Ps. 139:1–6, NLT)

Mia learned from her earliest days that God sees everything, so when her mom read the psalm we just read, she thought about the many things he knows: my heart, everything about me, where I am and what I'm doing, my thoughts, and my words. She thought about other parts of the Bible that talk about how God sees the whole earth (2 Chron. 16:9), knows our needs (Matt. 6:32), and even knows the future (Isa. 46:9–10).

Sometimes, Mia thought the fact that God knows everything as a negative thing. She thought he was constantly catching her doing and thinking bad things, so she told her mom, "I don't like that God knows everything. That means he even knows when I am thinking bad things."

"That's true," her mom replied, "but if you feel that way, you don't really believe Jesus loves you. If you know he truly loves you, then the fact that he is all-knowing is a wonderful thing. You can trust that he knows what has happened to you, what is happening to you, and what will happen to you. Even the bad things you think are wrapped in the fact that Jesus loves you perfectly.

"So your fears of God knowing your thoughts are blown away like the seeds of a dandelion in a strong wind. They disappear as you learn to rest in the fact that no matter what you have to face, Jesus is there with you, understands what you are going through, and will never abandon you. And God will always be wise in all he does in your life."

As Mia got ready for school, she thought, *God, you know everything, and that's a good thing for me because you love me even when I have bad thoughts and do the wrong thing. Thank you for that.*

⇒ Does knowing that God knows everything make you feel good or bad?
⇒ Why do you feel that way?
⇒ After today's reading, tell me why God's knowing everything can help you when you are afraid?

Prayer

Father, thank you that nothing takes you by surprise. You are never startled or taken off-guard. You always know what is going to happen and you surround that knowledge with your love and care. Keep that close to my heart and mind today.

Day 17: Who Is God?
All-Powerful

Scripture Reading

"Where were you when I laid the earth's foundation?
   Tell me, if you understand.
Who marked off its dimensions? Surely you know!
   Who stretched a measuring line across it?
On what were its footings set,
   or who laid its cornerstone—
while the morning stars sang together
   and all the angels shouted for joy?" (Job 38:4–7, NIV)

Miguel was going through a hard time. He and his parents had just moved to Chicago from Mexico, so he was living in a new place, trying to make new friends, and trying to speak good English. Miguel was a smart boy, so he caught on quickly, but even with his best efforts he had an accent that made it hard for some kids to understand what he was saying. So, American kids made fun of him and began to pick on him in other ways too. He hated it and began to be afraid to go to school. He began to complain to his parents and they took him in to see their pastor, who listened and understood.

Then the pastor read the verses we read today. Miguel thought the pastor, and God, was being mean to say such things. But then the pastor said, "The fact that God is all-powerful pretty well squashes any fear, anxiety, or worry. A God who laid the earth's foundations is big enough to handle anything that can cause you to be afraid. And even better, God is always good and wants good to come out of your time at school. Ask him to chase away your fears."

The next day when Miguel went to school and someone began to make fun of the way he talked, he just smiled. He knew God cared about his words and his thoughts and valued each one. That was enough for him.

⟹ Has anyone ever made fun of you?
⟹ How did that make you feel?
⟹ How might knowing that God is all-powerful help you the next tie someone makes fun of you?

Prayer
What a mighty, powerful God you are! Fill my heart and mind today with how you rule over all things—even the things I am afraid of. Remind me when I am afraid today that you have everything under your control.

Day 18: Who Is God?
Just

Scripture Reading

We ought always to thank God for you, brothers and sisters, and rightly so, because your faith is growing more and more, and the love all of you have for one another is increasing. Therefore, among God's churches we boast about your perseverance and faith in all the persecutions and trials you are enduring.

All this is evidence that God's judgment is right, and as a result you will be counted worthy of the kingdom of God, for which you are suffering. God is just: He will pay back trouble to those who trouble you and give relief to you who are troubled, and to us as well. This will happen when the Lord Jesus is revealed from heaven in blazing fire with his powerful angels. (2 Thess. 1:3–7, NIV)

Amelia's favorite thing to say is, "That's not fair!" She said it when her sister got invited to a birthday party, when her friend got to go to Disney World, and when her twin brother got an A on a test they both took. She always felt like everyone else was getting something better than she was, so life always felt unfair.

But one day something happened at school that she was certain was not fair. Someone made fun of her because she said she believed in God. They acted as if she was saying she believed that dragons and unicorns existed, and told her she was stupid if she believed in someone she couldn't see. But she knew she was right—God does exist and she does believe in him.

When she told her dad about the incident at school and how that made her afraid to go back to school again, he read the verses we read today. When he finished, Amelia asked, "So how does the fact that God is just help me with my fear of talking to this friend again?"

Her dad answered, "We know God will never abuse power; he will never act selfishly or in a way that doesn't make sense. He will always act with purpose and out of his love for you. You do not have to fear anyone or anything because in the end, Jesus will make everything right. So when you see this person at school tomorrow, keep in mind that God sees you and will always do the right thing by you. When you feel life is unfair or you fear your future will be unfair, know that all things will be made right in God's time and way—and that should take care of your fear of this person."

⇒ Has anyone ever made fun of you for believing in God?
⇒ What do you think you should say to someone who does that?
⇒ How can knowing that God will eventually make all things right help you when that happens?

Prayer

Lord Jesus, we long for the day you will come and make all things right. We know there will be all sorts of unfairness in the meantime, yet you are not only aware of them but anxious to correct them. Come, Lord Jesus!

Day 19: Who Is God?
Never Changing

Scripture Reading
In the beginning you made the earth.
  And your hands made the skies.
They will be destroyed, but you will remain.
  They will all wear out like clothes.
And, like clothes, you will change them.
  And they will be thrown away.
But you never change.
  And your life will never end
Our children will live in your presence.
  And their children will remain with you. (Ps. 102:25–28, ICB)

Gabe came home from school worried. His teacher had talked about how the planet is in trouble and how we are using up all the earth's resources. Gabe began to be afraid that everything was going to fall apart, so he asked his mom about it when he got home.

His mom read the verses we just read and said, "As solid as our planet seems, it will pass away. The end of the earth is treated as casually as a change of clothes in this passage—however, as depressing as this information is, the psalmist goes on to say of God, 'But you never change. And your life will never end.'

"The fact that God never changes is particularly important concerning his purposes and his promises. He will never be thwarted in his plans or tempted to break his promises. He can be counted on."

Gabe asked, "So how does that help me? I'm still afraid."

His mom thought about that for a minute and said, "God will not abandon his plans for us and for the world. As our passage concludes, 'Our children will live in your presence. And their children will remain with you.' Another version says, 'their children will live in security.'

"So as you go about your day, remember that God will never change and rest secure in the fact that you are connected to such a powerful and unshakeable being. Nothing can change or shake him."

⇒ What are some things you are afraid of will happen to the earth?
⇒ Why are you afraid of that?
⇒ Why does knowing that God never changes help you with that fear?

Prayer

Lord, I am in awe of you since you not only made the heavens and the earth but will outlast them for all of eternity. Thank you that I can count on you to never change your promises or your purposes. That allows me to release my fears to your charge and care.

Day 20: Who Is God?
Merciful

Scripture Reading

Lord, tell me your ways.
  Show me how to live.
Guide me in your truth.
  Teach me, my God, my Savior.
  I trust you all day long.
Lord, remember your mercy and love.
  You have shown them since long ago.
Do not remember the sins
  and wrong things I did when I was young.
But remember to love me always
  because you are good, Lord. (Ps. 25:4–7, ICB)

Mercy is not a word we think much about these days, so Harper wondered what it meant that the Bible verse today said, "Lord, remember your mercy." She continued to think about that as she walked to school. When she went inside and sat down at her desk, she noticed there was a new boy in class. The teacher introduced him as Eli.

Eli seemed to have trouble with the rules. He talked out of turn, left his desk and walked around the room, and even stepped in front of someone else in the lunch line.

Toward the end of the day, Harper was upset with Eli and wished the teacher would correct him. She was so angry about it, she pushed him out of the line at the end of the day when he started to step in front of her. However, instead of the teacher talking to Eli about it, she pulled Harper aside.

"Harper, I know it seems that Eli is not following the rules and that can be frustrating. But it's his first day and his mother told me he is having a hard time leaving his old school and is frightened about starting here. So, I decided to let things go today while he settles in. I'm asking you to have patience with him too."

Harper thought about this as she walked home. Suddenly, it hit her that the teacher was showing Eli mercy. That's what it means! He was doing things wrong, but she was not cracking down on him because he was frightened. It helped her to understand that God is merciful. He doesn't wait for her to mess up and pounce on her. Instead, he is patient and gives her time to learn and grow, which made her very glad.

⇒ Can you think of a time when someone showed you mercy when you didn't deserve it? Tell me about it.
⇒ How did that mercy make you feel?
⇒ How can knowing that God is merciful help take away your fears?

Prayer

Heavenly Father, you truly are loving, compassionate, and merciful. I should never fear being perfectly open and honest with you. Fill me with confidence in your willingness to accept me, even with all my flaws, and take away any fear that threatens my relationship with you.

Day 21: Who Is God?
Gracious

Scripture Reading

"But our ancestors were proud and stubborn, and they paid no attention to your commands. They refused to obey and did not remember the miracles you had done for them. Instead, they became stubborn and appointed a leader to take them back to their slavery in Egypt. But you are a God of forgiveness, gracious and merciful, slow to become angry, and rich in unfailing love. You did not abandon them..." (Neh. 9:16–17, NLT)

God gives us a clear picture of how gracious he is in how he dealt with the Hebrews when he led them out of Egypt. In spite of his miraculous deliverance, they refused to trust him and even wanted to return to slavery in Egypt. Nevertheless, God was "gracious and merciful, slow to become angry, and rich in unfailing love."

The great news for us is that if God was so patient and gracious with a group of people who utterly abandoned him, he will be even more gracious with us as we try to follow him but occasionally fail in our efforts. It also means that our fears and anxieties will disappear like water poured onto hot desert sand. We can be confident that God will give us as many chances as we need to get it right. He will never ignore our efforts or refuse to meet us in our helplessness.

Being gracious is connected to God's mercy, so in our story yesterday, Eli's teacher was gracious to him as well as merciful. Someone has said that mercy is not getting what we do deserve and grace is getting something we don't deserve. Eli deserved to be disciplined for breaking the rules, but his teacher didn't do that, so she showed him mercy. She also gave him something he didn't deserve, which was asking Harper to go easy on him. That was gracious.

So as you come across something today that makes you afraid, keep in mind that God is gracious and let him chase away any fears that attack you, as you stand firm in his love.

⇒ When has someone been gracious to you (giving you something you didn't deserve)?
⇒ Parent, share a time when God has been gracious to you.
⇒ How does knowing God is gracious help take away your fears?

Prayer

Thank you for being gracious, O God. I am grateful that I never need fear that you will be impatient with me or refuse to help me when I ask. Your divine grace is beyond my ability to understand it, and you have said that you will help me when I call. I ask for that assistance today.

Day 22: Who Is God?
Spirit

Scripture Reading

[Jesus said,] "If you love me, you will do the things I command. I will ask the Father, and he will give you another Helper. He will give you this Helper to be with you forever. The Helper is the Spirit of truth. The world cannot accept him because it does not see him or know him. But you know him. He lives with you and he will be in you.
"I will not leave you all alone like orphans. I will come back to you. In a little while the world will not see me anymore, but you will see me. Because I live, you will live, too. On that day you will know that I am in my Father. You will know that you are in me and I am in you. He who knows my commands and obeys them is the one who loves me. And my Father will love him who loves me. I will love him and will show myself to him."(John 14:15–21, ICB)

At this point in the Gospel of John, Jesus reassures his disciples that he is not abandoning them. As he encourages them, he also lifts our hearts with the wonderful assurance, "I will not leave you all alone like orphans." How is he making sure they, and we, are not left alone? His Father is sending a Helper, the Spirit of truth to be with all believers.

This passage goes with what Jesus said earlier, in John 4:24 (NIV): "God is spirit, and his worshipers must worship in the Spirit and in truth." Because God is spirit, he can accompany and guide us in a way that a merely physical being could not. He can walk with us through our fears and help us face our anxious thoughts. According to this passage, he will help us obey his commands, which we want to do because we love him. This reassures us that no matter what troubles us, he will help us look at it the right way and help us to know what to do.

Today, memorize the sentence, "He lives with you and he will be in you." Then, as you face whatever scares you today, be certain that the mighty God who created and rules the universe is living in you through his Holy Spirit.

⟹ How is having the Holy Spirit with us like having Jesus with us all the time?
⟹ How can the Holy Spirit be with us in a way that another person cannot?
⟹ How does that help you when you are afraid?

Prayer

Wow, God! You not only love me, but that you give your Holy Spirit to walk with me each day. Thank you that no matter what happens, I know that you are with me, caring for me.

Day 23: Who Is God?
Awesome

Scripture Reading

"Listen to this, Job;
  stop and consider God's wonders.
Do you know how God controls the clouds
  and makes his lightning flash?
Do you know how the clouds hang poised,
  those wonders of him who has perfect knowledge?
You who swelter in your clothes
  when the land lies hushed under the south wind,
  can you join him in spreading out the skies,
  hard as a mirror of cast bronze?

"Tell us what we should say to him;
  we cannot draw up our case because of our darkness.
Should he be told that I want to speak?
  Would anyone ask to be swallowed up?
Now no one can look at the sun,
  bright as it is in the skies
  after the wind has swept them clean.
Out of the north he comes in golden splendor;
  God comes in awesome majesty.
The Almighty is beyond our reach and exalted in power;
  in his justice and great righteousness, he does not oppress.
Therefore, people revere him,
  for does he not have regard for all the wise in heart?" (Job 37:14–24, NIV)

Today we use the word *awesome* so casually it has lost its meaning. When Sebastian went to see the mountains for the first time, he declared, "This is awesome."

His sister said, "You always say that about everything you like."

Sebastian looked again at the Rockies and said, "This *is* awesome. Nothing I earlier said was awesome really is."

His sister, who was older, thought that's the way she feels when she understands God's power and majesty. She realized that God is awesome in a way that nothing and no one else has ever truly been.

The writer of our passage compares how awesome God is to what it is like to look at the sun. We all know it's so bright we can't look at it for very long. As it says, "The Almighty is beyond our reach and exalted in power."

So what does this have to do with our fear? It means anything we are afraid of is so powerless in comparison to God that it is almost useless. Nothing can stand against God's awesomeness.

When you encounter something you are afraid of today, remember that "God comes in awesome majesty" and rest in confidence that nothing can defeat him. You are safe in his care.

⇒ How might thinking about God as awesome help you the next time you are afraid?
⇒ Even though God is awesome, we don't have to be afraid of him. Why is that? (Because we know he loves us.)

Prayer

Father, I thank you that you define the word *awesome* and that everything else pales in comparison to you. Help me to remember that you come in awesome majesty for my sake. You are my friend, not my enemy, so all my fears can be chased away in your presence.

Day 24: Who Is God?
Holy

Scripture Reading

"You must faithfully keep all my commands by putting them into practice, for I am the LORD. Do not bring shame on my holy name, for I will display my holiness among the people of Israel. I am the LORD who makes you holy. It was I who rescued you from the land of Egypt, that I might be your God. I am the LORD." (Lev. 22:31–33, NLT)

Chloe was feeling anxious because today she was trying out for the basketball team. She wasn't sure she was good enough to make it, but she loved basketball and hoped for it with all her heart. The idea that she might not make it was making her stomach hurt.

Each morning Chloe's dad read to her. Today's reading was from the book of Leviticus, and Chloe was having trouble with all the laws the Lord told Israel to obey. She didn't understand why there were so many laws and why it mattered to God what people ate and wore.

But when her dad read the passage we read today, something else stood out to her. Three times in these few sentences, God said, "I am the Lord." Maybe that was why they had so many laws. Perhaps God wanted them to daily remember that they were different from everyone else because they had him as their God.

Chloe thought about what God is like. She knew he was loving, kind, wise, gracious, and so on. She could think of people who had those kind of qualities too. Did she know anyone who is holy? Not in the way God is, that's for sure! He is the only truly holy one she could think of.

Thinking about that made her fears about basketball drift away. As she went to the try-outs, she asked God to surround and protect her with his holiness. "Lord, I know nothing can change the way you love and care for me, because you are the only holy one and you never change. I really want to be on this basketball team, but I know whether I make it or not, you are there with me—and that makes all the difference."

⇒ Is something making you anxious today the way Chloe was worried about the basketball try-outs? If so, tell me about it.

⇒ How did knowing that God is holy help Chloe?

Prayer

Holy God, I thank you that you are above everything that causes me to fear. You are much greater than that which is causing me anxiety. Help me to keep that confidence throughout my day and to remember who you truly are.

Day 25: Who Is God?
Provider

Scripture Reading

"No one can serve two masters. For you will hate one and love the other; you will be devoted to one and despise the other. You cannot serve both God and money.

"That is why I tell you not to worry about everyday life—whether you have enough food and drink, or enough clothes to wear. Isn't life more than food, and your body more than clothing? Look at the birds. They don't plant or harvest or store food in barns, for your heavenly Father feeds them. And aren't you far more valuable to him than they are? Can all your worries add a single moment to your life?

"And why worry about your clothing? Look at the lilies of the field and how they grow. They don't work or make their clothing, yet Solomon in all his glory was not dressed as beautifully as they are. And if God cares so wonderfully for wildflowers that are here today and thrown into the fire tomorrow, he will certainly care for you. Why do you have so little faith?

"So don't worry about these things, saying, 'What will we eat? What will we drink? What will we wear?' These things dominate the thoughts of unbelievers, but your heavenly Father already knows all your needs. Seek the Kingdom of God above all else, and live righteously, and he will give you everything you need.

"So don't worry about tomorrow, for tomorrow will bring its own worries. Today's trouble is enough for today." (Matt. 6:24–34, NLT)

Amelia thought about two things almost constantly: *What am I going to eat today?* and *What am I going to wear today?*

From the moment she got up, she thought about how to get out of eating things she didn't like and how she could manage to eat as much as possible of what she did like. This usually meant a battle with her parents.

And what to wear was even more consuming. She wanted to wear clothes that the other girls would like so that she wouldn't seem weird or strange. She also hoped they would like her more because of the amazing things she wore. So, each morning she ended up changing clothes many times because she was afraid the other girls would make fun or her or, worse, not pay attention to her at all. When she woke up in the morning, she felt anxious right away because this decision was so difficult for her.

So, when Jesus talked about not worrying about what we should eat and what we should wear, it got her attention. Amelia realized she worried about that all the time!

She decided to take Jesus at his word, and she clung to the phrase, "he will give you everything you need." That meant Jesus would help her to know he loves her, even if the other girls make fun or her or ignore her. That day Amelia decided to try something new. She would wear the first thing she tried on and not keep changing her clothes. She would trust Jesus to take care of her, even if other girls were mean. She knew Jesus would give her everything she needs.

⇒ Do you have any fears about what you eat? If so, what are they?
⇒ Do you have any fears about what you wear? Tell me about that.
⇒ Does Jesus words about not worrying about our food and clothes help you? Why or why not?

Prayer
Father, help me to trust you even when I am afraid. You have promised to give me everything I need, so I trust you to help me not be worried about what I eat or wear. Help me to trust you, not money or things.

Day 26: Who Is God?
Transcendent

Scripture Passage
Who else has held the oceans in his hand?
  Who has measured off the heavens with his fingers?
Who else knows the weight of the earth
  or has weighed the mountains and hills on a scale?
Who is able to advise the Spirit of the Lord?
  Who knows enough to give him advice or teach him?
Has the Lord ever needed anyone's advice?
  Does he need instruction about what is good?
Did someone teach him what is right
  or show him the path of justice?
No, for all the nations of the world
  are but a drop in the bucket.
They are nothing more
  than dust on the scales.
He picks up the whole earth
  as though it were a grain of sand. (Isa. 40:12–15, NLT)

Transcendent is not a word we use very often (perhaps you've never before heard it). The Merriam-Webster Dictionary defines transcendence as "extending or lying beyond the limits of ordinary experience." Sebastian's experience in the Rockies was like that when he said the mountains were awesome. It pulled him into feeling something he'd never felt before.

However, when we speak of God being transcendent, it goes beyond this. He is, by definition, beyond the limits of ordinary experience. As today's passage says, "Who else has held the oceans in his hand? Who has measured off the heavens with his fingers?"

What does that mean for our fears? It means that no matter what we fear, we trust a God who is above and beyond anything life can throw at us. He's above everything that scares us and is unaffected by it. As our passage says, "Did someone teach him what is right or show him the path of justice?"

God knows what you fear and has already made plans to make it right. Nothing can stop him because he is transcendent. As you go about your day, keep the phrase "Who else knows . . . ?" in mind each time you come up against something you feel you can't handle. Realize that there is no one else like the Lord who knows and has power over all things.

⇒ After today's lesson, what would you say it means that God is transcendent?
⇒ How can the fact that he is transcendent help you with your fears or the things that make you feel anxious?

Prayer

Father God, help me to realize how truly different you are from any other person I know. You never do anything wrong, and you are all-wise and powerful. Help me to rest in that today as I trust you with my fears.

Day 27: Who Is God?
Healer

Scripture Reading

All that I am, praise the Lord.
　Everything in me, praise his holy name.
My whole being, praise the Lord.
　Do not forget all his kindnesses.
The Lord forgives me for all my sins.
　He heals all my diseases. (Ps. 103:1–3, ICB)

Wyatt has cancer, so when he read that God "heals all my diseases," it got his attention. Cancer had scared him more than anything else ever had, so he wondered what it meant to his fears that God is a healer?

Wyatt knew that not everyone was healed. Just a few months earlier when he was in the hospital, he'd lost a good friend, John, to cancer. So he asked his dad what did the psalmist meant when he said God "heals all my diseases"?

His dad thought about it for a bit before he answered. Finally, he said, "One way to look at it is that God does eventually heal. Your friend John is now healthier than he has ever been in heaven. But I know that's not what you mean. And I'm not sure that's what the psalmist means either."

"So what does it mean?" Wyatt asked again

"Think of all the illnesses or accidents you've recovered from throughout your lifetime, Wyatt. There are probably more of them than you can count. Generally, God heals. Now that you have a more serious disease, you should assume God is going to heal you. And in the meantime as you go through treatments, you can praise the Lord as this psalm says. That will help you remember that he is in control, even of your health."

His dad then paused and added, "I will pray that with you. Let's remind each other."

> ⇒ Have you ever been afraid of being sick, or known someone close to you who has that fear?
> ⇒ Why should we assume God is going to heal us?
> ⇒ How does praising God help us with our fears?

Prayer

Thank you, God, that you are the healer. Let all my fear go away since I know that. Help me to praise and to trust you completely instead of fearing what might happen to me. I want you, not my sickness, to be my focus. Help me in this. I can't do it alone.

Day 28: Who Is God?
Victorious

Scripture Reading

Jesus asked, "Do you finally believe? But the time is coming—indeed it's here now—when you will be scattered, each one going his own way, leaving me alone. Yet I am not alone because the Father is with me. I have told you all this so that you may have peace in me. Here on earth you will have many trials and sorrows. But take heart, because I have overcome the world." (John 16:31–33, NLT)

Haven hated being alone. She didn't like being alone in her bedroom at night. She didn't like being home alone when she first got home from school. But most of all, she didn't like being away from her family at camp, where she felt really alone even when she was surrounded by people.

The first night at camp, she was homesick, but they had lots of activities and she was surrounded by people, so she felt all right and even looked forward to the week. However, the second day, some of the girls teased her and said they didn't want her in their cabin. That made her terribly homesick, and she wished she could call her mom to come get her. She thought the girls were mean, which frightened her enough to go talk to her counselor.

The counselor said she would talk to the girls, but she also read the passage we just read and Haven thought when Jesus said, "Here on earth you will have many trials and sorrows. But take heart, because I have overcome the world" that he was talking directly to her.

It also encouraged her that Jesus felt lonely. Yet, that loneliness didn't stop him. And he knew he wasn't alone because the Father was with him. She knew the Father was also with her.

The conflict with the girls at camp seemed like a fierce battle, but Haven could see that it was just a tussle. By the end of the week, she had made peace with the girls and with future fears of being alone.

⇒ Do you like to be alone? Why or why not?
⇒ Have you ever felt lonely when you were with a lot of people? Tell me about it.
⇒ In what way are we never alone?

Prayer

Jesus, I'm so glad you have already told us the end of the story. You cannot lose, so Satan, the world, and mean people hold no power over me. I am so grateful. Let me not forget it for a moment.

Day 29: Who Is God?
Angry

Scripture Reading

You have recorded my troubles.
   You have kept a list of my tears.
   Aren't they in your records?
On the day I call for help, my enemies will be defeated.
   I know that God is on my side.
I praise God for his word to me.
   I praise the Lord for his word.
I trust in God. I will not be afraid.
   What can people do to me? (Ps. 56:8–11, ICB)

Max had a step-brother who was always angry. That made him afraid to be around him, because he was never sure what would happen. His brother had hit him in anger before, and he often yelled at him, even if Max wasn't doing anything wrong. He felt it was just best to stay away from him.

That's why when his pastor talked about God's anger being a good thing, Max had trouble with that idea. Because of his step-brother, he thought someone who was angry was out of control and using his or her anger as a weapon to lash out at those around them.

So he asked his mom about it when he got home from church. She told Max that God's anger is nothing like most of the anger he had experienced. She explained that anger can be good, such as when a person is angry at someone for being cruel to someone else. That anger may be what is needed to stop the mean person from hurting others. Or perhaps anger will make us change bad laws that hurt people instead of help them. But she also explained that all human illustrations fall short; these examples give us a glimpse of anger as it should be, but it is still imperfect because all human anger is tainted by sin. We cannot separate who we are from how we feel.

"That is not true of God," she said. "He is not a slave to his own emotions as we are. Even when we are angry for all the right reasons, we have to question our fury because it so easily runs away with us and becomes our master. This can never happen to God. He is master of all, never mastered by anything."

"So do I need to be afraid of God?" Max asked.

"No, that's the great thing," his mother answered. "God always has our back. He knows what threatens us and his anger burns against all evil. We don't have to be afraid at all."

⇒ Ask your mom or dad to tell you about a time they were angry for the right reason.
⇒ Now ask them to tell you a time when they were angry for the wrong reason.
⇒ What is the difference?
⇒ Why do we never have to be afraid of God?

Prayer

God, I thank you for your anger, because it is perfect and never unfair. I pray you would help me to know your anger is not against me, since you see Jesus Christ, who is perfect, rather than my sins. That means your anger is only against those who are against you. Because of that, I rest in your love and protection, secure in you.

Day 30: Who Is God?
Comforter

Scripture Reading

All praise to God, the Father of our Lord Jesus Christ. God is our merciful Father and the source of all comfort. He comforts us in all our troubles so that we can comfort others. When they are troubled, we will be able to give them the same comfort God has given us. For the more we suffer for Christ, the more God will shower us with his comfort through Christ. (2 Cor. 1:3–5, NLT)

Brooklyn was afraid of bad things happening. She worried all the time about what each day would bring. What if she couldn't do the obstacle course they had to do in gym class? What if that mean girl bothered her at recess? What if she failed the test she had in math? What if she picked up germs in the bathroom and got sick? On and on went Brooklyn's worries.

But what an encouraging passage we read today, and what a good glimpse of who God is. He is "our merciful Father and the source of all comfort." And "the more we suffer for Christ, the more God will shower us with his comfort through Christ."

So what does that mean for Brooklyn's fears, worries, and anxieties? It means that no matter what happens to her, she can know that in allowing it, God is merciful. He's not mean or harsh, but gentle and kind. He is also there to comfort her when she faces hard things.

In love Isaiah 51:12, the Lord says, "I am the one who comforts you. So why should you be afraid?"

⇒ What one thing are you most afraid of when you think about your day?

⇒ Why does that thing make you afraid?

⇒ How might our passage help you not to be afraid?

Prayer

Thank you that you are my perfect Father. You will never be harsh or unfair. You will never make me pay the full penalty of my sins, but will always show mercy. Your arms are open wide, waiting to comfort me. Help me to recognize that as I go through this day.

Day 31: Who Is God?
Blesser

Scripture Reading

When Jesus saw his ministry drawing huge crowds, he climbed a hillside. Those who were apprenticed to him, the committed, climbed with him. Arriving at a quiet place, he sat down and taught his climbing companions. This is what he said:

"You're blessed when you're at the end of your rope. With less of you there is more of God and his rule.

"You're blessed when you feel you've lost what is most dear to you. Only then can you be embraced by the One most dear to you.

"You're blessed when you're content with just who you are—no more, no less. That's the moment you find yourselves proud owners of everything that can't be bought.

"You're blessed when you've worked up a good appetite for God. He's food and drink in the best meal you'll ever eat.

"You're blessed when you care. At the moment of being 'care-full,' you find yourselves cared for.

"You're blessed when you get your inside world—your mind and heart—put right. Then you can see God in the outside world.

"You're blessed when you can show people how to cooperate instead of compete or fight. That's when you discover who you really are, and your place in God's family." (Matt. 5:1–9, MSG)

(Parents: We are going to do something different in this devotional. With each beatitude, you will share an example from your own life or ask your child to share an example.)

This section of the Bible is called the Beatitudes and is from what is called Jesus' "Sermon on the Mount." Jesus talks about each of these things as being a blessing, but every one of them sounds hard. We're going to talk about each thing he said to get a better idea of what it means.

"You're blessed when you're at the end of your rope. With less of you there is more of God and his rule." (*Parent, tell your child a time when you were at the end of your rope and God helped you.*)

"You're blessed when you feel you've lost what is most dear to you. Only then can you be embraced by the One most dear to you." (*Ask your child*): Can you think of a time when you were sad and someone helped you feel better? Tell me about it. (*When the child is finished, ask*): How can God make us feel better when we are sad?

"You're blessed when you're content with just who you are—no more, no less. That's the moment you find yourselves proud owners of everything that can't be bought." (*Parent, tell your child about a time you were content and why that is such a good way to be.*)

"You're blessed when you've worked up a good appetite for God. He's food and drink in the best meal you'll ever eat." (*Ask your child*): How is God better than the best meal you've ever had?

"You're blessed when you care. At the moment of being 'care-full,' you find yourselves cared for." (*Parent, tell your child about a time when you cared for another and that made you feel good.*)

"You're blessed when you get your inside world—your mind and heart—put right. Then you can see God in the outside world." (*Ask your child*): What do you think it means to get your mind and heart put right? How does that help you understand God better?

"You're blessed when you can show people how to cooperate instead of compete or fight. That's when you discover who you really are, and your place in God's family." (*Parent, share a time that you helped someone cooperate instead of fight.*)

So when you feel afraid of something today, keep in mind what Jesus said it means to be truly blessed. When you feel scared or anxious, tell yourself, "I am blessed." That simple thought can turn things around.

Prayer

Jesus, you are the one who blesses. You take care of me all the time in ways I don't even think about. Help me to remember that you are always with me, and that you always want to help me. That's the best blessing I could possible have.

Day 32: Who Is God?
Head of All

Scripture Reading

The Lord is king. Let the earth rejoice.
  Faraway lands should be glad.
Thick, dark clouds surround him.
  His kingdom is built on what is right and fair.
A fire goes before him
  and burns up his enemies all around.
His lightning flashes in the sky.
  When the people see it, they tremble.
The mountains melt like wax before the Lord.
  He is Lord of all the earth.
The skies tell about his goodness.
  And all the people see his glory. (Ps. 97:1–6, ICB)

Chase was confused when his mom read this psalm. "God sounds scary!" he said when she finished.

"Why do you say that?" his mom replied.

Chase thought a second and then said, "Dark clouds surround him. He burns up his enemies. People tremble. Mountains melt. That's scary!"

His mother smiled and said, "I see what you mean." Then she handed the book to him and asked, "How does this psalm start?"

Chase read, "The Lord is king. Let the earth rejoice."

"So what does the person writing this psalm want us to know about God?"

Chase pondered that for a moment. "That God is in charge? And that's a good thing?"

His mom nodded. "I think you are on to something." Then she asked, "So what do those scary sounding things have to do with that idea?"

Chase shrugged. "I guess he wanted us to know how powerful God is." Then he paused and added, "And that means we'd better not mess with him."

His mom smiled. "True. We don't want to mess with God. But because we are loved and accepted by God through Jesus Christ, we don't have to be afraid of him. We can trust him to look out for us. Only those who are his enemies have to be afraid of him. His being in charge is a good thing for us."

Chase thought about that. "So the reason we don't need to be afraid of God's awesome power is because he is on our side. He will always come to our defense. Does that mean that bad things will never happen to us?"

"No, but it does mean that whoever did that bad thing has far more to fear than we do! God is the ultimate "big brother," a protector who has our backs. So we can let our fears drift away in the knowledge that nothing is out of his control. Nothing escapes his notice or takes him by surprise. In general, we can relax in the certainty that nothing can touch us without his permission."

⇒ Does this psalm make God sound scary to you? Why or why not?
⇒ If God is the king of everything, why is that a good thing?
⇒ How do you know God has your back no matter what happens?

Prayer

Help me to keep in mind that you are king of everything. As I face things that cause me to fear or feel anxious, let me rest in the confidence that you are in charge and that nothing gets past you. If the "mountains melt like wax" before you, then there is not a single thing on earth that can threaten me.

Day 33: Who Is God?
Jealous

Scripture Reading

Be careful. Don't forget the agreement of the Lord your God that he made with you. Don't make any idols for yourselves. The Lord your God has commanded you not to do that. The Lord your God is a jealous God. He is like a fire that burns things up." (Deut. 4:23-24, ICB)

Maria frowned as her dad read this passage. "It's hard to think about God being jealous, because isn't jealousy a bad thing?" she asked.

Her dad nodded. "It's a very bad thing for we humans. We hate jealousy in ourselves as we see the way it tears us apart inside. We hate it in those we love because we feel smothered and controlled by their jealousy. This is another of those traits that only God can manifest correctly."

"How is God different from us? Maria asked.

Her dad said, "God is not just a bigger version of ourselves—he is completely and utterly different from us since he never sins." He paused and then asked Maria, "Why are you usually jealous of another person?"

After thinking a moment, Maria answered, "They have something I want or I wish I was more like them in some way."

"Exactly," her dad said "You compare yourself to others and somehow feel inadequate. God is not in any way inadequate. Rather, he is completely self-sufficient and has no lack or need. God is jealous not because he fears he is not measuring up, but because he knows that without him we are rudderless and headed for darkness and destruction."

That was his concern for the nation of Israel in this passage. If they simply settled in with the godless cultures around them, they would soon adopt the horrendous customs those people practiced, such as child sacrifice, temple prostitution, and brutal slavery. They would drift farther and farther from God, who is the only light in this world and the only hope we have for anything good in life and for all eternity."

Maria asked, "So what does this mean for my fears? Won't it just make them worse, since I we know I am falling short of God's expectations?" Her dad replied, "Absolutely not, because God's jealousy reaffirms his great and powerful love for us. He doesn't want to share us with other gods because he knows they are false gods who will destroy us. He knows that following anyone other than him leads to unhappiness and sorrow. By his jealousy he wants to spare us from that."

⇒ How can the fact that God is jealous about his relationship with you help your fears?

⇒ Why is it safe to run to God for protection in spite of the fact that he's a jealous God?

Prayer

Thank you, Lord, for being jealous for my affections. Thank you for the certainty that I can only find happiness in you. Fill my heart and mind with that confidence as I encounter things that frighten me today. Help me to know without a shadow of a doubt that you are the safe place for me.

Day 34: Who Is God?
Tender

Scripture Reading
[Zechariah's prophecy at John the Baptist's birth]:

"Praise the Lord, the God of Israel,
  because he has visited and redeemed his people.
He has sent us a mighty Savior
  from the royal line of his servant David,
just as he promised
  through his holy prophets long ago.
Now we will be saved from our enemies
  and from all who hate us.
He has been merciful to our ancestors
  by remembering his sacred covenant—
the covenant he swore with an oath
  to our ancestor Abraham.
We have been rescued from our enemies
  so we can serve God without fear,
in holiness and righteousness
  for as long as we live.
And you, my little son,
  will be called the prophet of the Most High,
  because you will prepare the way for the Lord.
You will tell his people how to find salvation
  through forgiveness of their sins.
Because of God's tender mercy,
  the morning light from heaven is about to break upon us,

to give light to those who sit in darkness and in the shadow of death,
and to guide us to the path of peace." (Luke 1:67–79, NLT)

Easton was in a bad mood. It had been a tough day at school and he was glad to get home. But when he got home, his mother asked him to finish doing a chore he'd neglected.

"I don't want to do that right now. I've had a terrible day. I'm tired and just want to be left alone!" he yelled.

Usually such a rude response to a reasonable request would have meant swift and immediate discipline, but that day his mother reacted in a way that caused him to be much more repentant than if she'd carried out her typical punishment.

"I'm sorry you had a bad day," she responded gently and kindly. "I suppose the chore can wait another day."

Her kind reaction made Easton thoroughly ashamed of yelling at his mom. He immediately changed his tune, as he wanted to respond to the tenderness she was showing him.

"Is it okay if I wait to the chore after dinner?"

"Of course," his mother replied.

Later that evening when his mom read today's passage, Easton mentioned his mother's behavior being like God's mercy. She replied, "My response is a very poor illustration of God's tenderness toward us. Many times I ignore, defy, or respond ungratefully to God—more times than I can possibly count. Yet God shows me tender mercy. That means that when I am afraid, he is safe. He is tender and will care for me no matter what life throws at me."

That makes me think of another verse As it says in Zephaniah 3:17 (NLT):

With his love, he will calm all your fears.
He will rejoice over you with joyful songs."

⇒ Can you give an example of how God is merciful to you?
⇒ Today, as you encounter things that make you anxious, how can the knowledge of "God's tender mercy" fill you with peace?

Prayer

Heavenly Father, I am grateful beyond words that you deal tenderly with me. I need your kindness and gentleness to wrap me in security so I can trust you with every difficult thing in my life. Help me to remember that today, and to be confident I have a safe place to land in your tenderness.

Day 35: Who Is God?
Heavenly

Scripture Reading

I trust in the Lord for protection.
So why do you say to me,
    "Fly like a bird to the mountains for safety!
The wicked are stringing their bows
    and fitting their arrows on the bowstrings.
They shoot from the shadows
    at those whose hearts are right.
The foundations of law and order have collapsed.
    What can the righteous do?"
But the Lord is in his holy Temple;
    the Lord still rules from heaven.
He watches everyone closely,
    examining every person on earth.
The Lord examines both the righteous and the wicked.
    He hates those who love violence.
He will rain down blazing coals and burning sulfur on the wicked,
    punishing them with scorching winds.
For the righteous Lord loves justice.
    The virtuous will see his face. (Ps. 11, NLT)

Aurora lived in a tough neighborhood. Fights and thefts were pretty common. She never went anywhere alone and felt nervous even when she was with others.

Because of that, she liked Psalm 11. It comforted her to know that God rules from heaven. She knew from his vantage point, he sees things we cannot see and understands what we cannot grasp. His view (and control) of what is happening is complete, while her knowledge is stinted and small. This psalm helped her gain a glimpse of the totality of God's knowledge.

Psalm 11 begins with total chaos. *Little has changed in 3,000 years,* Aurora thought. *God alone is my protection, because I can't count on human institutions. They will always disappoint me.*

So on Sunday morning when her pastor read this psalm, he asked, "So what can the righteous do?"

Aurora waited to hear the answer.

The pastor went on to say, "We can know that 'the Lord is in his holy Temple; the Lord still rules from heaven.' The certainty that he is a heavenly being who is above the fray is enough to give us peace and confidence. He will judge those who love wickedness, and the 'virtuous will see his face.' Or, as *The Message* puts it:

'God's business is putting things right;
he loves getting the lines straight,
Setting us straight. Once we're standing tall,
we can look him straight in the eye.'"

This means that when we are frightened and worried, we can run to God for refuge, knowing that with his heavenly perspective, he will bring order to chaos and accomplish his larger plan, of which we are mostly ignorant. Nevertheless, we can trust him and depend on his care for us."

Aurora thought about this as she returned to her neighborhood. She kept thinking about the phrase "the Lord still rules from heaven." She wanted that knowledge to take root in her heart to give her confidence that nothing is out of his control or takes him by surprise.

⇒ Where are you most afraid and why?
⇒ How does knowing that the Lord still rules from heaven help your fear of that place?

Prayer

There is a reason we call you our Heavenly Father. I am grateful that you are above all that goes on down here on earth. Nothing takes you by surprise, and you alone see the whole picture. Help me to trust you with the things I am afraid of. Thank you that you rule from heaven over all that happens here on earth.

Day 36: Who Is God?
Pray-er

Scripture Reading

Meanwhile, the moment we get tired in the waiting, God's Spirit is right alongside helping us along. If we don't know how or what to pray, it doesn't matter. He does our praying in and for us, making prayer out of our wordless sighs, our aching groans. He knows us far better than we know ourselves … and keeps us present before God. That's why we can be so sure that every detail in our lives of love for God is worked into something good.

God knew what he was doing from the very beginning. He decided from the outset to shape the lives of those who love him along the same lines as the life of his Son. The Son stands first in the line of humanity he restored. We see the original and intended shape of our lives there in him. After God made that decision of what his children should be like, he followed it up by calling people by name. After he called them by name, he set them on a solid basis with himself. And then, after getting them established, he stayed with them to the end, gloriously completing what he had begun. (Rom. 8:26–30, MSG)

Walter listened closely as his Sunday school teacher read this passage of Scripture. As always, when his teacher read the Bible, Walter was full of questions, so he asked, "What is the difference between God and his Spirit?"

Fortunately, Walter's teacher loved his questions. "I'm glad you asked, Walter! We cannot forget that God is three-in-one. That means the Holy Spirit is as much God as are the Father and the Son. All three persons of the Trinity are clearly reflected in this passage.

"When we believe in Christ, God gives us his Spirit so we will never be alone or feel abandoned. He doesn't tell us to gut it out on our own. Instead, he offers himself as a constant guide."

Walter thought about that as someone else asked, "Does the Spirit really pray for us like it says in those verses?"

The teacher nodded. "A huge part of his presence is that he prays for us, 'making prayer out of our wordless sighs, our aching groans.' That means if we are sad, anxious, or afraid—maybe so frightened that we can't even form words—the Holy Spirit turns our sighs and groans into a prayer for exactly what we need."

This got Walter's attention and made him ask another one. "Is that because he knows us better than we know ourselves?"

"Yes!" the teacher answered. "The reason God the Spirit can pray for us is that he knows us intimately, and is even praying for us in the way we need him to so that we can become more like Christ."

Later that day, Walter's parents had to leave him alone for a short while. He grew frightened when household noises clunked around him, but then he thought, *God himself is praying for me!* and those fears drifted away.

⇒ How does knowing that God the Spirit prays for you give you courage?

⇒ Why is it great to know that he prays for you even when you don't have the words?

Prayer

I love that you know my thoughts before I even say them aloud. And if I can't find the words, you even supply those. What a wonderful God you are! I am grateful that you never abandon me but always surround me with your Spirit to guide and care for me. Help me to remember that today.

Day 37: Who Is God?
Bountiful

Scripture Reading

Oh, visit the earth,
  ask her to join the dance!
Deck her out in spring showers,
  fill the God-River with living water.
Paint the wheat fields golden.
  Creation was made for this!
Drench the plowed fields,
  soak the dirt clods
With rainfall as harrow and rake
  bring her to blossom and fruit.
Snow-crown the peaks with splendor,
  scatter rose petals down your paths,
All through the wild meadows, rose petals.
  Set the hills to dancing,
Dress the canyon walls with live sheep,
  a drape of flax across the valleys.
Let them shout, and shout, and shout!
  Oh, oh, let them sing! (Ps. 65:9–13, MSG)

Zoey loved to shout and sing, so this psalm made her happy. It made her feel like yelling at the top of her lungs was okay to do. Maybe Mom was right when she suggested she do it outside instead of in, since this psalm was all about the outdoors.

Someone once asked Zoey where she feels closest to God. She didn't even have to think about it, but immediately answered, "When I'm outside." There was something about how big it is that made her soul swell in her. When she looked around at what God made, from the huge sky to the tiny wildflower, she definitely noticed earth's "dance," mentioned in this psalm.

Zoey thought back to last week when a good friend hurt her feelings. She felt very sad as she walked home on that hot summer day. She was afraid of parting ways with her friend. But then it began to rain, softly at first, and then it became a downpour. She began to run to get home faster, and as she ran in the pouring rain, she began to laugh and talk to God. "Thank you, God, for this rain," she yelled. "Let it wash away my fears of losing my friend. I love you!"

Somehow yelling that prayer healed something in her. No matter what her friend did, she was going to be okay.

⇒ How does looking at God's creation help you better understand who he is?
⇒ How can noticing God's creation, help take away your fears?
⇒ Have you ever been so happy that you shouted out your prayers to God? If so, tell me about it. If not, what might help you do that sometime?

Prayer

Creator God, I love the world you have made and am in awe of your creative power. As I come across things that make me fearful and anxious today, I pray that you will remind me of what a generous, good God you are. I pray my fears will flee in knowing that.

Day 38: Who Is God?
Greater

Scripture Reading

No one has seen God, but Jesus is exactly like him. Christ ranks higher than all the things that have been made. Through his power all things were made—things in heaven and on earth, things seen and unseen, all powers, authorities, lords, and rulers. All things were made through Christ and for Christ. Christ was there before anything was made. And all things continue because of him. He is the head of the body. (The body is the church.) Everything comes from him. And he is the first one who was raised from death. So in all things Jesus is most important. God was pleased for all of himself to live in Christ. And through Christ, God decided to bring all things back to himself again—things on earth and things in heaven. God made peace by using the blood of Christ's death on the cross. (Col. 1:15–20, NLT)

Lincoln was afraid of spiders. Most people think spiders are creepy, but he was terrified of them. Just seeing one sent him running the other way.

So when Lincoln read these verses, there were a few things that caught his attention. First of all, he thought about the fact that God made everything. That meant he even made spiders, and since everything God does is good, there must be some good reasons for them.

The second thing that made him stop and think was that Jesus is greater than anything in creation. That meant that Jesus was much greater than spiders, and much greater than Lincoln's fear of spiders. *After all,* Lincoln thought, *if I fear spiders, or anything else, for that matter, I'm seeing only a small part of what God is doing in the bigger picture. There are all sorts of things going on that I know nothing about. He is working out his plan that includes making peace with everything in heaven and on earth. What, then, could I possibly fear?*

So the next time Lincoln saw a spider, he still felt a shudder go through him, because he would never like spiders, but he didn't run.

⇒ Is there something that makes you so frightened that you panic and run?

⇒ Do you think you should be afraid of that thing? Why or why not?

⇒ Even if you are afraid or don't like something, how can you trust that Jesus is greater than your fear when you feel afraid?

Prayer

Lord, I am grateful that you not only made the earth and the heavenly realms, but are also greater than it all. Nothing is outside of your purpose and power. The fear I feel never touches you, because you feel no anxiety about it. Help me to rest in that knowledge and to let your Holy Spirit's confidence flow through me today.

Day 39: Who Is God?
Generous

Scripture Reading

Once Jesus was in a certain place praying. As he finished, one of his disciples came to him and said, "Lord, teach us to pray, just as John taught his disciples."

Jesus said, "This is how you should pray:

"Father, may your name be kept holy.

May your Kingdom come soon.

Give us each day the food we need,

and forgive us our sins,

as we forgive those who sin against us.

And don't let us yield to temptation."

Then, teaching them more about prayer, he used this story: "Suppose you went to a friend's house at midnight, wanting to borrow three loaves of bread. You say to him, 'A friend of mine has just arrived for a visit, and I have nothing for him to eat.' And suppose he calls out from his bedroom, 'Don't bother me. The door is locked for the night, and my family and I are all in bed. I can't help you.' But I tell you this—though he won't do it for friendship's sake, if you keep knocking long enough, he will get up and give you whatever you need because of your shameless persistence.

"And so I tell you, keep on asking, and you will receive what you ask for. Keep on seeking, and you will find. Keep on knocking, and the door will be opened to you. For everyone who asks, receives. Everyone who seeks, finds. And to everyone who knocks, the door will be opened.

"You fathers—if your children ask for a fish, do you give them a snake instead? Or if they ask for an egg, do you give them a scorpion? Of course not! So if you sinful people know how to give good gifts to your children, how much more will your heavenly Father give the Holy Spirit to those who ask him." (Luke 11:1–13, NLT)

When Grace read Luke 11, she thought about it for a long time. Jesus' disciples asked him to teach them to pray, and he taught them what we now call the "Lord's Prayer." Then Jesus then told a story about someone who gives another person what they ask for just because they keep on pestering him. What did that mean as she tried to stop being afraid all the time?

She asked her older sister what she thought. "I think Jesus was saying that even humans will respond when we ask them for things, but that our Father God is far more generous than any human, even a devoted parent."

Grace thought a moment and asked, "So what does it mean when it says he gives the Holy Spirit to us if we ask? Why do we need God's Spirit?"

Her sister answered, "The Holy Spirit will be with us every moment of the day; he will always be aware of our needs; and he is more generous than anyone we know on earth. We ask God for bread, and he gives us bread, but he also gives us himself. Wow!"

Grace pondered this a moment, then said, "So what does that have to do with my fears?"

Grace's sister hugged her and said, "It means you are never abandoned. You are always in God's company through his Spirit, and because of that he is always aware of your needs, and your fears. He will care and provide for you as you trust him with the details of your life."

Grace thought about that for a long time. "Lord, teach me to pray" she said. "And help me to let go of fear and anxiety because I know you are caring for me."

⇒ Do you talk to God all day long as you come across things that concern you? If not, why not?

⇒ How can talking to him about everything help you overcome your fears?

Prayer

Heavenly Father, thank you for giving me your Holy Spirit, who will be with me every moment and who will be generous with me in ways I can't even imagine. Help me to be thankful instead of scared.

Day 40: Who Is God?
Perfect

Scripture Reading

"Lord, you are loyal to those who are loyal.
 You are good to those who are good.
You are pure to those who are pure.
 But you are against those who are bad.
You save those who are not proud.
 But you make humble those who are proud.
Lord, you give light to my lamp.
 The Lord brightens the darkness around me.
With your help, I can attack an army.
 With God's help, I can jump over a wall.
The ways of God are without fault.
 The Lord's words are pure.
He is a shield to those who trust him.
Who is God? Only the Lord.
 Who is the Rock? Only our God.
God is my protection.
 He makes my way free from fault." (2 Sam. 22:26–33, ICB)

When his dad finished reading these verse, Elliot asked him, "Who is saying this?"

His dad answered, "This passage is an excerpt from a song David sang to the Lord on the day God rescued him from Saul and other enemies. I love that about David—after a horrible day, he takes time to compose a song of praise to God. I want to learn from his example."

Elliot thought about that. "So David was saying that God honored him and protected him from Saul, who wasn't listening to God."

"That's right," his dad nodded.

Elliot couldn't help but think of the bully who kept bothering him at school. David said that God is a shield to those who look to him for protection. He's also a solid rock, a fortress.

"Dad, what does it mean that God makes my 'way free from fault'"?

His dad answered, "That doesn't mean everything will always be hunky dory in our eyes, but it does mean that he is using whatever circumstances come our way to mold us and make us faithful, pure, and filled with integrity. Because he is perfect, he is continually perfecting us. So what could we possibly fear?"

Elliot liked that!

⇒ Are you afraid of someone? If so, who?
⇒ Should you be afraid of that person? Why or why not?
⇒ How can God help you not to be afraid of that person?
⇒ How does knowing that God is perfect help you as you face your fears?

Prayer

Lord, I know I will never be perfect as you are, but I am so glad you never give up on me as you move me away from my fears and anxieties into your perfection.

Final Thoughts

I hope dwelling on who God is for 40 days has helped your children move past their fears and rest in his love and goodness. My prayer for your child is that she will never go back to being as frightened and anxious as she was before taking this time to undo any faulty ideas she had about God and replacing them with the truth: that she is cared for by the Creator of the universe who will never leave her or abandon her.

If you found help through this book, pass it on to others who may need it and give it a good review on Amazon, or wherever you bought it. And if you would like a longer devotional that follows this format, check out my book **Proverbs for Kids**.

About the Author

Besides this book, JoHannah Reardon has written a family devotional and many novels. Check out all her books and follow her blog at **johannahreardon.com**; on Facebook at **JoHannah Reardon—freelance writer**; on Twitter at @johannahreardon; and on Pinterest.

Family Devotionals:
- ❖ *Proverbs for Kids*
- ❖ *No More Fear for Kids*

Devotionals:
- ❖ *No More Fear: 40 days to overcome worry*
- ❖ *Undone by Majesty and Mystery*

Blackberry County Chronicles:
- ❖ *Crispens Point—Book 1*
- ❖ *Cherry Cobbler—Book 2*
- ❖ *Prince Crossing—Book 3*

Distant Shores Series:
- ❖ *Redbud Corner—Book 1*
- ❖ *Highland Path—Book 2*
- ❖ *Gathering Bittersweet—Book 3*

Mystery:
- ❖ *Summerville* (A Maggie & Tim mystery)

Fantasy/Fairy Tale:
- ❖ The Land of Neo Trilogy

Made in the USA
Lexington, KY
21 February 2019